A Place to Talk

OUTSIDE

Elizabeth Jarman

Featherstone

Education

Reprinted 2010
Published 2009 by A&C Black Publishers Limited
36 Soho Square, London W1D 3QY
www.acblack.com

ISBN 9781408114896
Text © Elizabeth Jarman
Photographs © Elizabeth Jarman

A CIP record for this publication is available from the British Library.

Printed in the UK by Martins the Printers, Berwick-upon-Tweed

This book is produced using paper that is made from wood grown in
managed, sustainable forests. It is natural, renewable and recyclable.
The logging and manufacturing processes conform to the environmental
regulations of the country of origin.

To see our full range of titles
visit www.acblack.com

Contents

Introduction

The Bercow Review of Services for Children and Young People (0-19) with Speech, Language and Communication Needs (www.dcsf.gov.uk/bercowreview) describes speaking and listening as a life skill, and states that:

> 'The ability to communicate is an essential life skill for all children and young people and it underpins a child's social, emotional and educational development.'

The ICAN report[1] suggests that over 50% of children in England are starting school with some form of speech and language difficulty or disability.

The Early Years Foundation Stage reinforces that 'the development and use of communication and language is at the heart of young children's learning.'[2]

Professor Jim Rose, in his final report on the review of the primary curriculum, published in April 2009, www.dcsf.gov.uk/primarycurriculumreview, emphasises the need for a stronger focus on the teaching and learning of speaking and listening skills from the early years, to ensure that by the age of 7, in other words at the end of Key Stage 1, children will 'have a secure grasp of the literacy … skills they need to make good progress thereafter.'

More than 97% of schools nationally are now involved in the Healthy Schools Programme and over 70% have achieved National Healthy School Status. This translates to around 4 million children and young people. Children and young people in 'Healthy Schools' say that they feel healthier, happier and safer. Their parents say that they feel more involved in their child's health and learning and often feel better themselves. Schools say that the National Healthy Schools Programme has brought sustained improvement in behaviour, standards of work and school management. (See **www.everychildmatters. gov.uk/health/healthyschools**)

[1] Cost to the Nation, I CAN, 2006
[2] QCA/DfES: Curriculum Guidance for the Foundation Stage, p45

The Early Years Foundation Stage also puts emphasis on children as independent learners both inside and outside, and practitioners are encouraged to plan outdoor activities, as follows:

The outdoor environment

- Being outdoors has a positive impact on a child's sense of well-being and helps all aspects of their development.
- Being outdoors offers opportunities for doing things in different ways and on a different scale from indoors.
- It gives children first-hand contact with weather, seasons and the natural world.
- Outdoor environments offer children freedom to explore, use their senses, and be physically active and exuberant.

Para 3.3 Enabling Environments
(See **www.standards.dfes.gov.uk/eyfs/resources/downloads/3_3_ep.pdf**)

This book considers the significant role that the physical environment can play in supporting children's speaking and listening skills in supporting inquisitive, verbal experimentation i.e. not just answering questions!

It includes:

- a summary of some of the key environmental influences, collated from research studies
- lots of examples of what this can look like in practice
- questions to prompt action
- sign-posts to further information.

We hope that you will be challenged and inspired to create some really effective 'places to talk'.

OUTSIDE

Five environmental factors to consider

Following a review of research and practice in a wide range of Early Years settings, we have identified five really important environmental points to consider when creating spaces designed to encourage children's speaking and listening skills.

1 The physical environment should reflect the pedagogy[1] of the setting.

Establishing a clear understanding of your pedagogy will inform the way that you plan your learning environment. The way that a physical space is arranged says a lot to children about what is expected there and the sort of interactions welcome. It's really important that the learning environment and pedagogy connect and support one another.

2 Practitioners should make the most of the space available, both inside and out.

It's important to view learning spaces as a whole, including both inside and out and make the most of what's available. Across the space, children need secure spaces to talk where they feel comfortable and relaxed.

3 Spaces should take account of physical factors that can impact on learning e.g. noise, colour and light.

Noise

Being in a noisy environment all the time makes it really difficult for children to concentrate. This can have a negative effect on their speaking and listening skills.

Colour

Colours need to be chosen carefully as they can affect children's behaviour and ability to focus and engage in conversation.

Light

Current research confirms that we are all energized by natural sunlight and that children learn faster in spaces with natural light. Light can also be used to create mood and define an area.

4 The environment should not be over stimulating.

Too much choice can be overwhelming. Storage options should therefore be carefully considered. This can be particularly challenging in a home context where space might be limited.

5 Spaces should be viewed from the child's perspective.

Informed by a thorough understanding of how language develops, we should keenly observe what the children are actually doing and how they are responding to the spaces we create. This helps us to plan appropriate, flexible environments that stimulate speaking and listening skills and reflects their preferred contexts for learning.

[1] Pedagogy is your 'teaching' style.

Twelve ideas to try

Inspired by practice from many settings, we have created twelve 'places to talk' that reflect the five environmental factors.

Each idea is spread over a few pages:

- There is a 'starter' photograph of the space and a description of how we created it.

- We have included key points about why we chose those particular materials and why we positioned the furniture as we did.

- There are also photographs of children using the space, with their comments and teachers' observations of what they did.

- We have included some action points for you to consider.

You'll see that what we are suggesting doesn't have to cost a fortune, in fact you may already have some of the materials and resources that we've used. What it does involve though, is an informed view and keen observation skills which inform planning, so that you create the sort of environment that reflects what you want for children in your setting.

Whilst acknowledging that opportunities for speaking and listening are everywhere, we hope that these ideas will inspire you to review and develop some special 'places to talk' in your setting.

A space for 'small group' conversations

HOW AND WHY

This space was created in one of the quietest parts of the garden. We wanted to offer a contained, quiet space for just a few children to investigate resources together.

We hung a natural green canopy from a low branch and pegged open the entrance, inviting the children in. We used a tarpaulin on the floor and covered it with soft blankets and cushions to make it a comfortable place to sit.

Inside the space we added a small collection of interesting resources to investigate – shells, pebbles and cones. The resources were attractively presented in baskets. The careful choice of colours allowed the space to blend into the natural environment.

A small group of boys found the space and carefully went inside. They engaged immediately with the resources, which they were familiar with but not in this space. They spent a long time listening for the sea in the big shells. "Can you hear the sea?" "This one's got a bug in it." "I wish this was our house." They spent a long time inside the space, watching other children playing in other parts of the playground from a distance. They enjoyed having the space to themselves.

ACTION

Do you offer spaces for 'small group' conversations? Places where children can think, reflect and discuss?

OUTSIDE

Defined spaces presented with care

HOW AND WHY

Attractive edging has been carefully added to this collection of flowers and herbs. It has defined these small spaces. Much care has been taken to provide points of interest that encourage discussion, exploration that appeals to the senses – the feel, smell and look of the plants and natural resources. The space has also been enclosed with a rush roll adding to the fence. This blocks out the busy movement from the parallel playground.

The teacher had completed a noise audit inside the classroom and found that it was difficult for children to find a quiet space. By providing simple, natural resources outside the classroom in a small corner, the children enjoyed opportunities for reflection, stillness and maybe relaxed conversation.

ACTION

Think about the noise level in your setting. What opportunities do children have to focus more deeply in quieter spaces, natural areas and those that appeal to the senses? Are there underused areas outside that could be made into calm, reflective thinking and talking places?

OUTSIDE

Spaces for collections

HOW AND WHY

The practitioners noticed how much their children enjoyed making collections, particularly outdoors. Here, the feel, textures, smells and properties of natural resources provoked their questioning and wondering. The collections were often placed in different areas in the garden; sometimes the children remained there and created their own space with the resources and sometimes they relocated themselves in an area that they preferred.

To maximise on the learning potential, they provided children with a 'store' to house a range of items to support and extend this activity. They included an old suitcase, some interesting artwork, brooms and brushes, recycled household furniture and utensils.

Knowing they could leave resources and return to them meant the children's interest, exploration and collections could grow, extend, and become richer and more meaningful over a period of time. This offered deeply fulfilling opportunities for children to build their collections, sharing these, and making links and discoveries.

This sustained spoken language and gave opportunities for children to discuss what they noticed over time. Children's self-esteem was enhanced as they felt their resources were valued. They liked the control over their choice of materials and through observations the teacher was able to find out more about children's knowledge, understanding and preferences.

ACTION

Take a moment to really think about your environment from the child's perspective. How do you enhance confidence, interest, motivation and language? How do you show you value children's discoveries and findings and support their learning by giving opportunities for continued access and storage?

OUTSIDE

Blurring the edges of the space

HOW AND WHY

The outer perimeter of this school was developed into a pathway which took the children around the varied landscape; along the tarmac, through the trees, across the field and into the bushes!

Using natural landscapes such as paths and trees in gardens which draw the eye and create natural soft boundaries often adds a softness to the space and can provoke interest and further investigation. Finding spaces such as curving paths, holes in hedges, collections of trees which are all organic shapes, or bushes, shrubs and plants of interesting textures. Using natural areas of interest, even in the most urban areas, will pose questions to the children, which become a stimulus leading to further questioning and discussion.

Here, pathways were cleared in the bushes creating a very shady tree lined spot. This area allowed the children to watch people passing on the pathway above. It was a wonderful place to observe from.

Introducing a line of rocks into this space, full of fossils, added a wonderful visible border and a fascinating place for children to wonder and investigate.

Adding wind chimes and carving a line from a significant poem to this rock added a further point of interest and defined the purpose of the school site for visitors, staff and children.

ACTION

Walk around the boundaries of your site. How does it blend into the local community? Could you develop the boundaries, creating observation spaces and adding points of interest? How could you soften or enclose some stretches?

OUTSIDE

Spaces to gather

HOW AND WHY

This setting introduced lots of small spaces for children to gather naturally. On a limited budget, they accessed some free logs and employed a chainsaw artist to create several tables and chairs.

These 'places to gather' invited opportunities for talk. The location of these spaces was informed by observation of where children gathered naturally in the outside context. Positioning of seating was planned to encourage interaction and non-verbal communication.

A PLACE TO TALK

These boys gathered naturally in the bushes! Staff let the grass in this part of the garden near the bushes grow long and then cut pathways into the grass, leading into their favourite space. So much conversation went on in here!

OUTSIDE

A PLACE TO TALK

Simply adding these thin slices of wood drew the children.

Considered positioning of these tables facilitated discussion.

A simple space to gather and chat has been created with four logs around a fire pit. It provided a place for a few to gather informally, or a place for the whole group to come together.

In the far corner near the trees, staff added a collection of logs, which the children rolled and arranged to suit their play. Being away from the main group facilitated more private conversations.

ACTION

Where are children's preferred areas in your environment and how long do they spend there? How will this inform your future planning? Notice the common spaces where children naturally gather. How can you develop and resource these to trigger rich speaking and listening opportunities?

OUTSIDE

Well-presented resources to enhance outside provision

HOW AND WHY

In this very concrete small outside space, the practitioners introduced a variety of textured resources and equipment to extend their outside provision and inspire the children. They grouped the resources in big green buckets positioned on a pallet, to define the space. The children were not overwhelmed with too much choice. A careful selection of materials was on offer, most collected from the local builder's store and were free!

"Zoe look...bricks."
"They are heavy."

A PLACE TO TALK

"These are like rulers."

"Heavy wood. I can hold it with one hand though."

Within a risk-assessed environment, the availability of real materials like these added to the children's experiences and introduced real concepts of heavy and light, rough and smooth. They explored each container, touching, holding, expanding and replacing materials together.

ACTION

How do you extend your outside area? Do you offer the sorts of materials that will trigger inquisitive, curious language? How are these resources made available to the children to capture their interest?

OUTSIDE

A space round the corner

HOW AND WHY

The staff had carried out an audit to find out where children's preferred places for interaction were and the quality of the language used within these.

They noticed that some children naturally wanted to gather in spaces such as this one, away from the bikes and busyness of their outside area. Staff added some natural resources as a trigger for imagination, thought and focus. They put fabric over the top to add an enclosed and private feel and added bark to change the texture of the floor. They also added rush rolls to the railings blocking out road noise.

ACTION

Do you have any quieter spots where children can relax and not worry about fast moving bikes and scooters outside? Places where they can chat or maybe watch from?

Storytelling spaces

HOW AND WHY

This very grand old storytelling chair provides a wonderful place to sit, watch, talk and tell stories. The chair offers a security to the children. It has been there for generations! It is positioned in the corner of the garden, giving a good view of all that is taking place, but for the audience sitting listening to the storyteller, they are facing away from the motion and therefore not distracted.

This comfortable, informal, shady storytelling space makes use of an existing structure. The 'ceiling' has been lowered by draping a sheet over washing lines attached to the structure. It offers a place to retreat to, or somewhere for groups to snuggle and enjoy a story together! The calm colours set the scene for a more relaxed storytelling session.

ACTION

Where could you add some storytelling spaces in your garden? Think carefully about how the physical space itself could trigger speaking and listening between children and with groups at story time.

OUTSIDE

A child-height enclosed space

HOW AND WHY

This space was created using an upturned pallet box. We cut off some of the strips of wood, allowing a space for one or two children to crawl into. The slats allowed lots of natural light into the space but also provided shade. We used bath mats, blankets and some cushions to add comfort to the space and also included some clipboards, folders, paper and pens.

The playground lacked smaller semi-private spaces and so many children grouped round the edges. This observation informed the development and position of several small spaces, offering children the opportunity to spend time alone or with a small group of friends.

OUTSIDE

ACTION

Observe the places where children gather at playtime. Do you offer smaller, semi-private places for them to get away from the noise and often overwhelming action in the playground environment? Think about positioning when planning such spaces, developing the quieter places and areas that children are drawn to naturally, away from the busy flow of movement.

OUTSIDE

Secret spaces managed by the children

HOW AND WHY

These spaces were carefully created by the children as part of a project with Creative Partnerships. Children were given opportunities to choose their own interesting places to be, to investigate and to discover – to spend unhurried time talking with friends. Children were able to add resources and move them in their preferred ways. They discovered the interesting resources such as a bird box, wind chimes, magnifying glasses and wooden crates that had been attached to the fence and used these flexibly, often gravitating to them and using them as a natural space to gather and talk. The conversations in these spaces were free, uninhibited and secret!

ACTION

Look for existing places and resources that can be developed by children to enhance their opportunities to develop speaking and listening skills.

OUTSIDE

At the allotment

HOW AND WHY

Zoe and Oliver love spending time with their Grandad, Stan 'up the allotment'. Here they like digging, watering and talking. The space is defined by railway sleepers. It is a quiet outside space, away from road noise and a real contrast to their home garden space.

"What are these blue things for?"
"They keep the slugs away and stop them eating my plants."

"Can I eat this Grandad?"

ACTION

Even a small space can provide all kinds of real experiences for the children to draw on. Digging, planting, feeling and talking! Could you create a small growing space?

OUTSIDE

A bivvy in the garden

HOW AND WHY

Zoe and Oliver's dad regularly goes fishing and has a fishing bivvy. This space was set up to build on their interest and knowledge of fishing and their fascination about him fishing in the dark. We set up this bivvy, positioned so that it faced away from the activity in the garden. We added some battery operated lanterns and a rug. The space was very open ended and not over resourced.

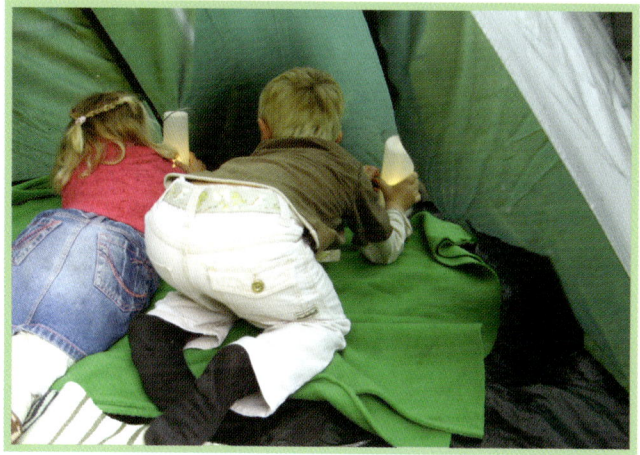

The colours used in this space took account of blending into the natural environment and the work of Dr. Max Luscher whose colour test indicated that greens are very relaxing.

Both Zoe and Oliver were quick to get into the space. Oliver was keen to take his wellies off in case he "messed it up." He was really drawn by the softness of the fleece we added. After exploring the internal dimensions of the space, both children were interested in the lanterns – switching them on and off.

They discovered that the lanterns worked best when they were held in the darkest part of the bivvy. They lay there, holding the lights, relaxed and chatting.

ACTION

Do you offer carefully resourced enclosed areas for children to explore and develop? Are there spaces that are open ended enough for them to add their own experiences? Are the spaces comfortable and positioned away from the main activity and motion in the outside area?

OUTSIDE

Action points

Here is a summary of the questions we posed to prompt action. Use them to reflect on the environment that you currently provide for children and then to help you focus on making positive changes.

Do you offer areas in the outside environment where 'small group conversations' can take place?

Think about the noise level in your setting. What opportunities do children have to focus more deeply in quieter spaces, natural areas and those that appeal to the senses? Are there underused areas outside that could be made into calm, reflective thinking and talking places?

Take a moment to really think about your environment from the child's perspective. How do you enhance confidence, interest, motivation and language? How do you show you value children's discoveries and findings and support their learning by giving opportunities for continued access and storage?

Walk around the boundaries of your site. How does it blend into the local community? Could you develop the boundaries, creating observation spaces and adding points of interest? How could you soften or enclose some stretches?

Where are children's preferred areas in your environment and how long do they spend there? How will this inform your future planning? Notice the common spaces where children naturally gather. How can you develop and resource these to trigger rich speaking and listening opportunities?

How do you extend your outside area? Do you offer the sorts of materials that will trigger inquisitive, curious language? How are these resources made available to the children to capture their interest?

Do you have any quieter spots where children can relax and not worry about fast moving bikes and scooters outside? Are there places where they can chat or maybe watch from?

Where could you add some storytelling spaces in your garden? Think carefully about how the physical space itself could trigger speaking and listening between children and with groups at story time.

Do you offer any child height spaces, comfortable ideal places for children to watch from, wonder and reflect?

Look for existing places and resources that can be developed by children to enhance their speaking and listening skills.

Even a small space can provide all kinds of real experiences for the children to draw on – digging, planting, feeling and talking! Could you create a small growing space?

Do you offer carefully resourced enclosed areas for children to explore and develop? Are there spaces that are open ended enough for them to add their own experiences to? Are the spaces comfortable and positioned away from the main activity and motion in the outside area?

Useful resources

The resources that we used to create our 'places to talk' were easy to source and inexpensive. They included:

- Blankets in natural, relaxing colours

- Textured cushions

- Different sized rugs

- Interesting objects to stimulate talk e.g. smooth stones, gnarled wood

- Battery operated push button lights

- Gazebo

- Logs

- Wicker baskets

- Fishing bivvys

- Bricks, gravel, pebbles, rocks

- Pallet

- Mosquito net

- A small number of carefully selected books

- A choice of writing and/or drawing materials

Further references and useful websites

The Communication Friendly Spaces Toolkit: Improving Speaking and Listening Skills in the Early Years Foundation Stage, ISBN: 1 85990 428 9 Elizabeth Jarman (2007) can be ordered from Prolog 0870 600 2400 and costs £14.95

Better Communication, 2008, can be downloaded from **www.dcsf.gov.uk/bercowreview**

Cost to the Nation, I CAN, 2006 available from **www.ican.org.uk**

Professor Jim Rose's Independent Review of the Primary Curriculum is available to download from **www.dcsf.gov.uk/primarycurriculumreview**

www.pge.com for information about day lighting studies on children's learning

www.sightlines-initiative.com for information about the Reggio Emilia's Children's Network, conferences and resources

www.quietclassrooms.org for guidance on controlling noise in settings and public places

www.colourtest.ue-foundation.org for information on the effects of colours on behaviour

Learning through Landscapes helps schools and early year's settings make the most of their outdoor spaces for play and learning **www.ltl.org.uk**

Forest Schools aim to encourage and inspire individuals of any age through positive outdoor experiences **www.forestschools.com**

Creative Partnerships is the Government's flagship creative learning programme, designed to develop the skills of young people across England, raising their aspirations and equipping them for their futures **www.creative-partnerships.com**

About the author

Elizabeth's background is in teaching.

Until 2006 Elizabeth was an Assistant Director at the Basic Skills Agency, working closely with the Skills for Life Strategy Unit and Sure Start Unit, DfES, DWP, leading the Step in to Learning Training and Development Programme.

More recently, Elizabeth developed the Communication Friendly Spaces™ Toolkit for practitioners and specializes in developing optimum conditions for learning.

See **www.elizabethjarmanltd.co.uk** for more information.

Thanks to all of the schools and practitioners who informed and inspired this publication, especially:

Foulsham Primary School, Norfolk
Emneth Children's Centre, Norfolk
Franworth Primary School, Nottinghamshire
St.Helens Montessori School, East Sussex
Sladefield Infants School, Birmingham
The Coombes Infant and Nursery School, Surrey
Paddock Wood Primary School, Kent
Oliver, Zoe and Grandad Stan